SCOOBY-DOO! SCIENCE Adventures

JINKIES!
The Mystery of States of Matter!

by Ailynn Collins

CAPSTONE PRESS
a capstone imprint

Published by Capstone Press, an imprint of Capstone
1710 Roe Crest Drive, North Mankato, Minnesota 56003
capstonepub.com

Copyright © 2025 Hanna-Barbera.

SCOOBY-DOO and all related characters and elements are trademarks of and © Hanna-Barbera. (s25)

Library of Congress Cataloging-in-Publication Data is available on the Library of Congress website.

ISBN: 9781669084662 (hardcover)
ISBN: 9781669084617 (paperback)
ISBN: 9781669084624 (ebook PDF)

Summary:
Stroll through a farmer's market with Scooby-Doo and Mystery Inc. to crack the case of states of matter! From melting ice cream to steaming hot drinks, witness the magical transformations that matter undergoes. Jam-packed with laugh-out-loud jokes, fascinating facts, and colorful illustrations, this Scooby-Doo! Science Adventure turns learning into a fun-filled investigation.

Editorial Credits
Editor: Donald Lemke; Designer: Tracy Davies; Media Researcher: Svetlana Zhurkin; Production Specialist: Whitney Schaefer

Image Credits
Getty Images: Aleksandr Zyablitskiy, 8, HappyKids, 17, Jenny Dettrick, 14 (bottom); Shutterstock: AlenKadr, 25 (plastic wrap), Andrei Armiagov, 13 (middle), Anton Starikov, 25 (bowl), baibaz, 15, barbaliss, 27 (sunglasses), Cartooncux (beaker), cover and throughout, Dark Moon Pictures, 29, DedMityay, 19, Designua, 7, 11, 26, Emil Timplaru, cover (ice cubes, puddle), Emir Kaan, 9, FoxGrafy, cover (evaporating puddle), Georgii Shipin, 22, HobbitArt (science icons), cover and throughout, kazoka, 16, leolintang, 10, Maria Martyshova (background), cover and throughout, Michael Ahanov, 12, MockupMonster, 25 (cup), ms.nen, 4, Muhammah Haseeb, 28, Nata-Lia, 6 (right), Nataliia ZH, 18, Nattapat.J, 27 (bottom), ND700, 21, Paul Orr, 27 (sunrise), Photoongraphy, 5, Platon Anton, 23, Radu Bercan, 14 (top), Ricardo Javier, 25 (salt), Shawn Hempel, 6 (left), Sommai, 25 (ice), Standret, 20, v74, 24, Valerio Pardi, 13 (back), Vitaly Krivosheev, 27 (TV)

Any additional websites and resources referenced in this book are not maintained, authorized, or sponsored by Capstone. All product and company names are trademarks™ or registered® trademarks of their respective holders.

Printed and bound in the USA. PO 6121

Table of Contents

INTRODUCTION
Disappearing Ice Cream 4

CHAPTER 1
Solids 8

CHAPTER 2
Liquids 12

CHAPTER 3
Gases 16

CHAPTER 4
Changes in States 18

CHAPTER 5
Plasma 26

Glossary 30
Read More 31
Internet Sites 31
Index 32
About the Author 32

INTRODUCTION

Disappearing Ice Cream

Scooby-Doo and the Mystery Inc. gang walk through a farmer's market on a sizzling summer day. The stalls are filled with eggs, fresh fruits and vegetables, and—most importantly—snacks!

Shaggy and Scooby each buy an extra-large ice-cream cone from a friendly vendor. As they walk away, their frozen treats immediately begin to shrink! Shaggy thinks he's found the gang's next mystery.

Shaggy's treat isn't disappearing, of course. It's changing states—states of matter, that is!

Everything around us is made of matter: frozen treats, fresh foods, school supplies, and even planet Earth. You are made of matter too! In fact, scientists say that matter is anything that has mass and takes up space.

FACT

Mass is the amount of matter that an object is made of.

Matter is made up of super tiny particles called atoms and molecules. These particles are like the building blocks of everything! They can form into all kinds of shapes and sizes.

Matter is found in three states: solid, liquid, and gas. For example, a cup is a solid, coffee is a liquid, and hot steam is a gas.

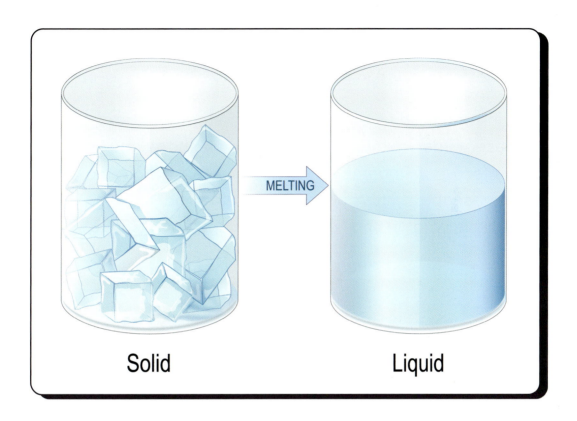

Matter can change states. Remember how Shaggy thought his ice cream was disappearing? It was changing states from a solid to a liquid. *Rikes* is right!

FACT
Changes in state usually happen in the presence or absence of heat.

CHAPTER 1

Solids

Think of a solid as one of the superheroes of matter. Why? Because solids are tough! They keep their shape and volume no matter what. Imagine trying to squeeze a rock into a different shape. . . . It's not budging, right? That's because solids have what we call a "definite shape and volume."

Inside a solid, things are pretty snug. Atoms and molecules (that's science-speak for tiny particles) are packed together like a can of yummy sardines. There's barely any room to wiggle! Each atom is locked in place next to its buddies—and everybody stays put.

In a solid state, particles have just a teensy-weensy bit of energy. They're not lazy, but they definitely don't move around much. This low energy means they stay close to each other and keep their shape.

Trying to reshape a solid like wood, metal, or plastic with your bare hands? Good luck!

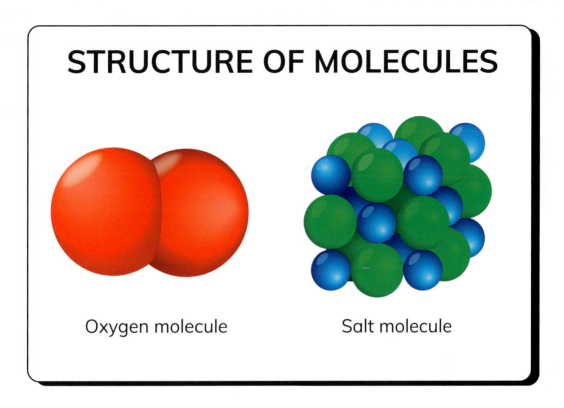

An atom is the tiniest piece of an element. It might be on its own or paired up with others. For instance, oxygen and helium can exist as just one atom. A molecule is when two or more atoms link up tightly. Salt, also known as sodium chloride, is a molecule made when sodium and chlorine atoms join forces.

CHAPTER 2

Liquids

Think of a liquid as the shape-shifter of the matter world. Liquids have a set volume, but they don't have a fixed shape. They're flexible!

The particles in a liquid are a bit more spaced out than in a solid. This gives them more energy to move around. The extra wiggle room allows particles to slide past each other, making liquids flow smoothly.

Like, why did the water get a job at the mystery shop?

Because it's great at taking the shape of things . . . just like a disguise!

This flexibility is why liquids can change into the shape of any container. If you pour water into a tall glass, it stretches up. Move it to a wide bowl, and it spreads out. It's the same amount of water, but the liquid changes form to fit its new space perfectly.

Examples of liquids: Think about water, oil, or milk. No matter their container, they adjust to fit! They're always ready for any shape they need to take.

Melting and Molding Chocolate

WHAT YOU'LL NEED:

3 small bars of chocolate—dark, milk, and white chocolate

3 bowls

small pot of hot water
(You'll need an adult's help here.)

sandwich bags

scissors

shallow cake pan

sprinkles (Optional, but who doesn't love a bit of extra sparkle?)

WHAT TO DO:

1. Break up each chocolate bar into its own bowl.
2. Place each bowl over the pot of hot water, one by one, to gently melt the chocolate. (Make sure an adult is nearby.)
3. Once the chocolate is all melty and smooth, scoop the white and milk chocolate into two separate sandwich bags.
4. Snip a tiny corner off each bag to make a small hole.
5. Use these DIY piping bags to squeeze out your own cool designs onto the bottom of the shallow cake pan. Add the sprinkles, if desired!
6. Cover your masterpiece with the melted dark chocolate, and let it cool in the refrigerator.
7. Once it's hard, flip the pan over, and pop out your chocolate creations. Check out the awesome designs you made!

The chocolate started as a solid, right? When heated, it turned into a liquid. That's because the heat made the chocolate particles move around so much that they couldn't hold their solid shape. But when you cooled the chocolate, those particles settled back into place. The chocolate became solid again!

Think about it: What other things change from solid to liquid when you heat them? How would you turn those liquids back into solids?

CHAPTER 3

Gases

Gases are the third state of matter. They don't have a fixed shape or volume. Instead, they expand to fill any container.

In gases, particles move quickly and have a lot of energy. This causes weak connections between them, allowing them to spread far apart.

FACT

Examples of gases include oxygen, carbon dioxide, helium, and steam.

Gases have more empty space between particles than liquids or solids. This is why we can walk through air without feeling it. Gases are also mostly invisible and expand to fill their containers completely.

For a quick demonstration, add baking soda to a bottle. Then pour in vinegar. Watch gas bubble up! Covering the top of the bottle with an uninflated balloon shows how gases expand to fill space.

CHAPTER 4
Changes in States

When temperature shifts, matter can change states. Just like ice cream and chocolate, solids melt at specific temperatures known as melting points. Different solids have different melting points.

The melting point of chocolate is about 97 degrees Fahrenheit (36.1 degrees Celsius). At that temperature, the solid chocolate will turn into a liquid.

The melting point of ice (or Scooby's ice cream) is 32°F (0°C).

A jeweler might melt gold. Its melting point is 1,948°F (1,064°C). That's hot! Iron melts at about 2,800°F (1,538°C).

When the heat is removed, liquids will often return to their solid states . . . if the temperature is right.

Water turns back into ice at the same temperature that ice melts into water. This is called the freezing point. In the same way, the chocolate turned back into a solid in the refrigerator.

    We see changes in the states of matter in our everyday life. When it rains, water comes down from the clouds. This is called precipitation. Water falls from the sky to the ground. Hail and snow are also types of precipitation.

    Once the rain passes and the hot sun shines again, the water in the puddles disappears.

The sun has dried up the puddles. We say that heat has caused the rainwater to evaporate. Water changes into vapor (or a gas) and rises into the sky.

It's cooler up there, so the vapor goes through condensation and turns back into a liquid.

Clouds are made of tiny droplets of water. As the clouds get full of water droplets, they fall back down to the ground as precipitation. Water then collects on the ground or in rivers, oceans, and ponds.

These four stages—evaporation, condensation, precipitation, collection—make up the water cycle. It's a never-ending circle. It happens all over the planet!

Not all solids become liquids before turning into gas. Carbon dioxide in its solid form is called dry ice. It's very cold and shouldn't be touched with bare hands.

When exposed to the warmer air, dry ice doesn't melt but goes from a solid state directly to a gas.

FACT

A solid that changes into a gas without melting into a liquid goes through a process called sublimation. There is no liquid form.

Experiment: Water Cycle

WHAT YOU'LL NEED:

salt
1 cup hot water
spoon
large clear bowl
mug
plastic wrap
ice

WHAT TO DO:

1. Mix salt into the cup of hot water and stir until dissolved. (You may need an adult's help to do this.)

2. Pour the hot salty water into the larger bowl. (This is like the ocean.)

3. Place the mug inside the large bowl. (This is the land.)

4. Cover the bigger bowl with plastic wrap. (The wrap is like the clouds in the cool sky.)

5. Place ice cubes on top of the plastic.

What you'll see: After several minutes, notice that the plastic wrap is damp on the inside. Remove the plastic wrap. Look at the water in the mug. This is the land that has been rained on. If you taste it, you'll notice it's not salty. This is how the water cycle works.

What do you think has happened?

CHAPTER 5

Plasma

We are all familiar with the three states of matter. But did you know there's a fourth state? It's called plasma!

Plasma is known as an exotic state of matter. It is formed under extreme conditions, such as high temperatures or with a lot of electricity.

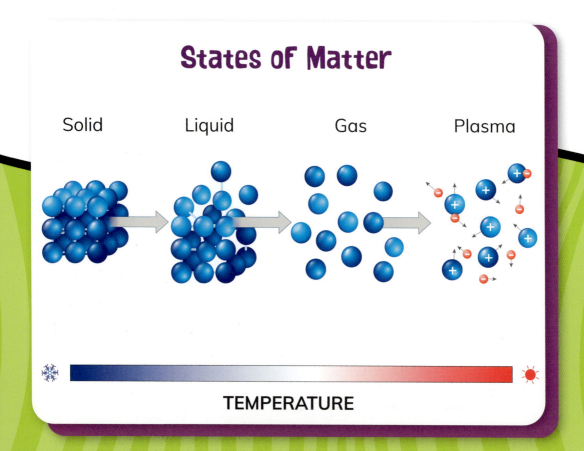

The particles in plasma have a lot of energy. They behave as if they have an electric charge.

Remember how everything is made of atoms? Atoms have tiny particles inside them called electrons, protons, and neutrons. When some gases are heated up or subjected to an electromagnetic field, their electrons are knocked away. The gas becomes plasma.

Plasma is found in stars like our sun. Lightning is a form of plasma. Some TVs also have plasma. We even use plasma to make neon signs!

A great way to see how plasma acts is to use a plasma ball. This ball has gases inside its sealed glass. Much of the air has been sucked out, making a vacuum. When the ball is turned on, the electricity charges the gas atoms inside. This creates plasma.

When you touch a plasma ball, "lightning" appears inside it. This lightning follows your fingertips. The electrons pass through you to the ground.

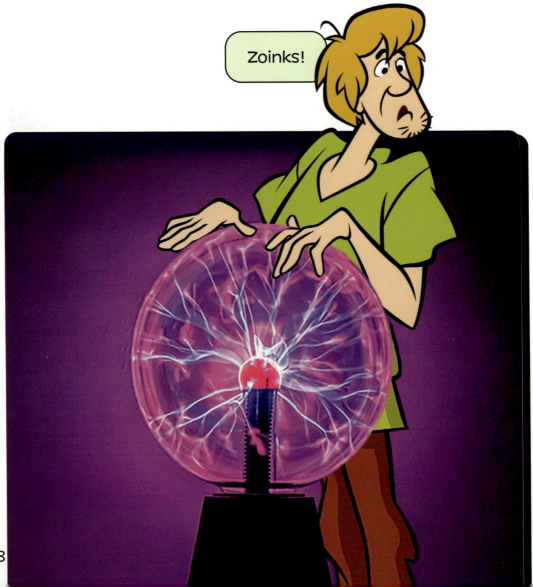

So, gang, we've learned a lot about the mysterious states of matter! From solids that stand strong, liquids that flow, gases that fill every space, and electrifying plasma. Just like our favorite mystery-solving team, science is all about curiosity and discovering the wonders around us.

Keep exploring, keep asking questions, and remember: The world is full of fascinating mysteries waiting for you to solve!

GLOSSARY

atom (AT-uhm)—the smallest piece of an element that can exist

condensation (kon-den-SAY-shun)—the process by which gas turns into a liquid

evaporation (ee-vap-uh-RAY-shun)—the process by which liquid turns into a gas

freezing (FREE-zing)—the process by which a liquid turns into a solid

mass (MAS)—the amount of matter something is made of

matter (MAT-uhr)—anything that has mass and takes up space

molecule (MOL-uh-kyool)—two or more atoms joined together

plasma (PLAZ-muh)—a state of matter with lots of energy, like in stars

solid (SOL-id)—state of matter that keeps its shape and volume

sublimation (sub-li-MAY-shun)—when a solid changes directly into a gas without becoming liquid

READ MORE

Claybourne, Anna. *Recreate Discoveries about States of Matter*. New York: Crabtree Publishing Company, 2019.

Emminizer, Theresa. *The Water Cycle*. New York: Enslow Publishing Inc., 2023.

Miller, Marie-Therese. *States of Matter: A Sesame Street Science Book*. Minneapolis: Lerner Publications, 2023.

INTERNET SITES

BBC: Bitesize: What Are the States of Matter?
bbc.co.uk/bitesize/articles/zsgwwxs

Britannica Kids: Matter
kids.britannica.com/kids/article/matter/353444

Ducksters: Solids, Liquids, and Gases
ducksters.com/science/solids_liquids_gases.php

INDEX

atoms, 6, 9, 11, 27, 28

condensation, 22, 23

evaporation, 22, 23

freezing point, 20

gases, 6, 16–17, 22, 24, 27, 28

helium, 11, 16

liquids, 6, 7, 12–13, 15, 19, 22, 24

matter, 5, 8, 12, 16, 18, 21, 26, 29

melting points, 19

molecules, 6, 9

plasma, 26–28

precipitation, 21, 23

solids, 6, 7, 8–10, 12, 15, 19, 20, 24

vapor, 22

volume, 8, 12, 16

water cycle, 23

ABOUT THE AUTHOR

Ailynn Collins has written many books for children, from stories about aliens and monsters, to books about science, space, and the future. These are her favorite subjects. She lives outside Seattle with her family and five dogs. When she's not writing, she enjoys participating in dog shows and dog sports.